Take off with

Bumblebee 3

Workbook

W0391722

Schroedel

Inhalt

Children from Europe

At school

The Union Jack

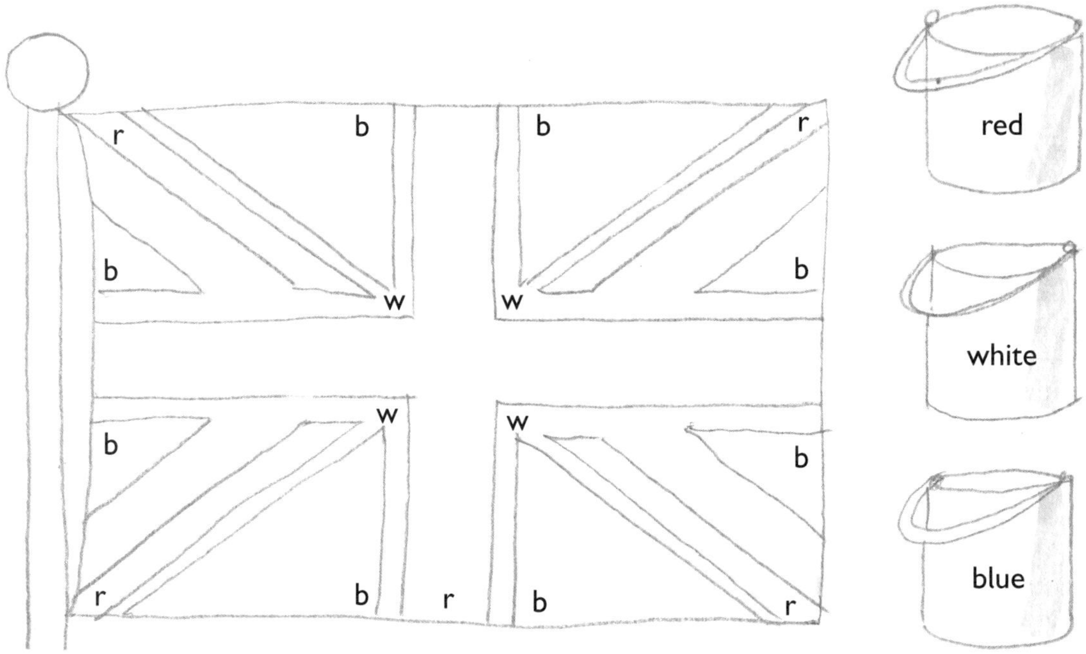

Colour the flag.

CD Saying hello

Who is talking? Listen and number.

That's me

CD

Who is talking? Listen and number.

I am happy

I am happy ☺.

I am eight.

I am a boy.

I am sad ☹.

I am nine.

I am a girl.

Read and match.

CD What I need at school

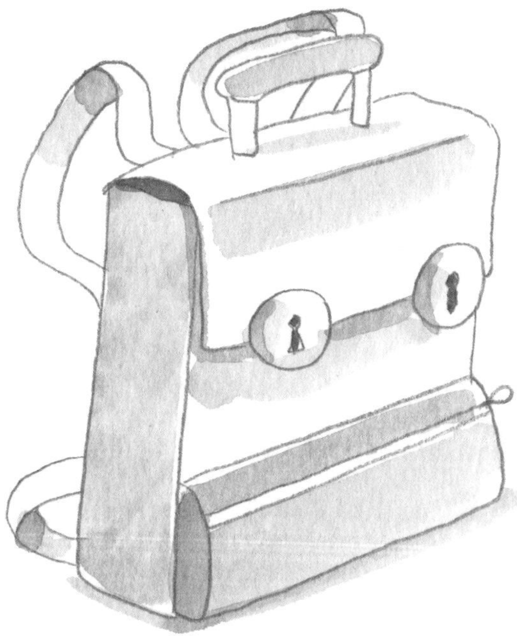

What is in Sue's schoolbag? Listen and draw or write.

What is in your schoolbag?

School talk

CD

Listen and number.

Colours and clothes

Colourful clothes

1. red **2.** green **3.** brown **4.** blue **5.** yellow
6. purple **7.** white **8.** black **9.** pink **10.** orange

Colour the words and clothes.

Colour word search

x	z	x	z	r	e	d	x	z	x	z	x	z	g	x
z	x	z	x	z	x	z	x	b	z	x	z	x	r	z
x	b	x	z	z	z	x	x	r	x	z	z	x	e	z
x	l	x	x	x	z	z	x	o	x	x	z	z	e	w
z	a	z	y	e	l	l	o	w	z	z	x	x	n	h
x	c	x	x	z	z	z	r	n	x	x	x	z	z	i
x	k	z	z	z	x	x	a	x	z	z	z	x	x	t
z	z	z	x	x	x	z	n	x	p	u	r	p	l	e
x	x	x	x	z	z	x	g	x	i	x	x	z	z	z
z	z	z	x	b	l	u	e	x	n	x	x	z	z	x
z	z	x	x	x	z	z	x	x	k	x	x	z	z	x

Find the words.

Our favourite colours

What does Simon say? What does Sue say?

Hide-and-seek

2 skirts

hats

dress

tie

jackets

pullovers

Find the clothes.

CD Pack the suitcase

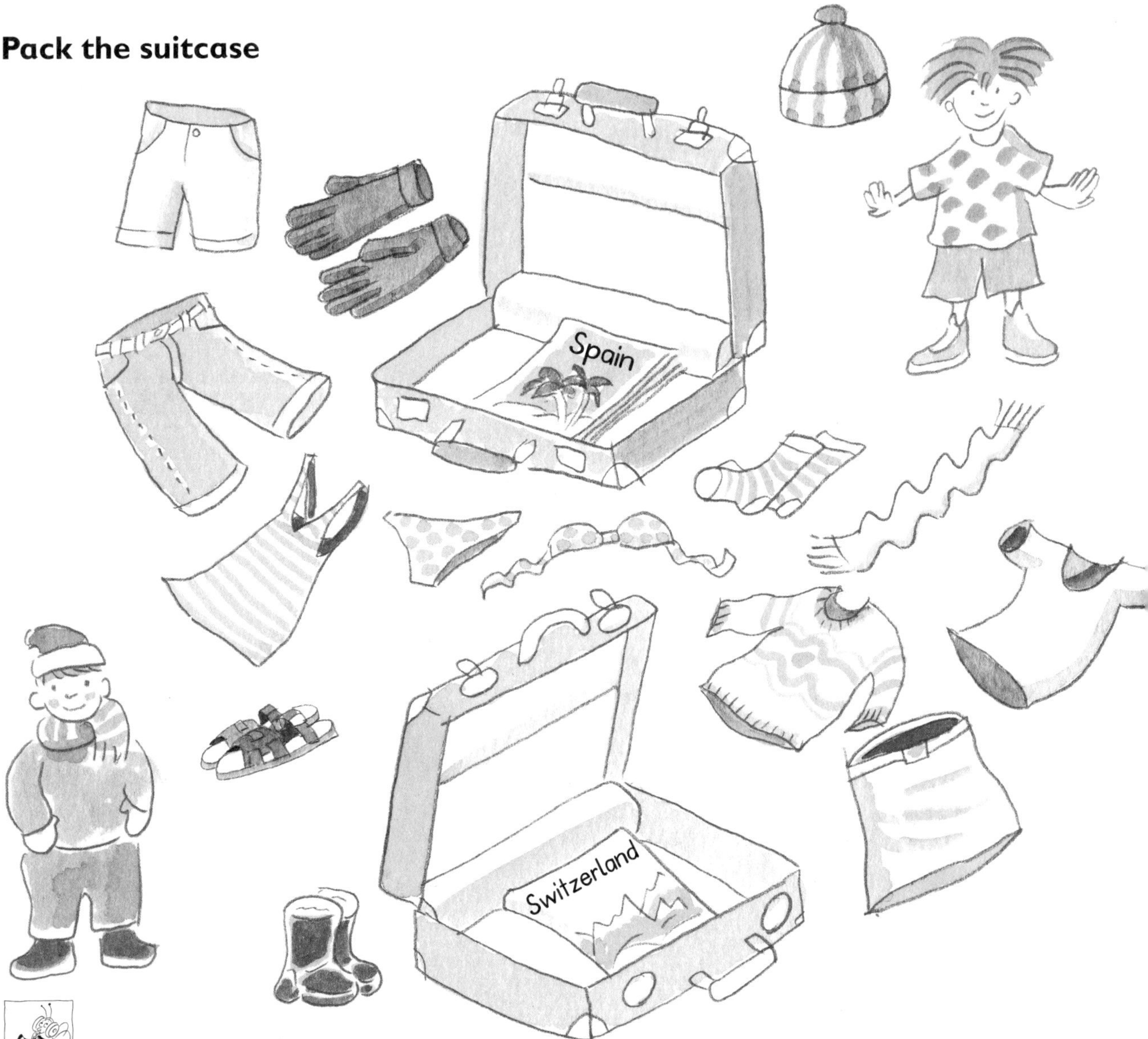

Listen and match.

Pack your suitcase for your holidays.

Outdoor game

Listen and

Can you w

Clothes that protect us

- knee pads
- cycle shorts
- helmet
- T-shirt
- shorts
- trainers
- elbow pads

Who wears what? Read and match.

Crazy school uniforms

Find a partner. Do a colour dictation.

Let u

Our favo

Int

CD Teddy bear, teddy bear

Teddy bear, teddy bear,

_____________ around.

Teddy bear, teddy bear,

_____________ the ground.

Teddy bear, teddy bear,

_____________ your head.

Teddy bear, teddy bear,

_____________ to bed.

Teddy bear, teddy bear,

_____________ the stairs.

Teddy bear, teddy bear,

_____________ some pears.

Teddy bear, teddy bear,

_____________ good night.

Teddy bear, teddy bear,

_____________ the light.

eat	go	shake	turn
jump	touch	say	turn out

Fill in the words. Number the pictures.

Outdoor games

CD

Listen and number the pictures.

Can you write the words?

CD Teddy bear, teddy bear

Teddy bear, teddy bear,

_______________ around.

Teddy bear, teddy bear,

_______________ the ground.

Teddy bear, teddy bear,

_______________ your head.

Teddy bear, teddy bear,

_______________ to bed.

Teddy bear, teddy bear,

_______________ the stairs.

Teddy bear, teddy bear,

_______________ some pears.

Teddy bear, teddy bear,

_______________ good night.

Teddy bear, teddy bear,

_______________ the light.

eat	go	shake	turn
jump	touch	say	turn out

Fill in the words. Number the pictures.

Let us play together!

CD

Listen and number the pictures.

What happens next?

Animals

Do you know the animals?

dogs

rabbits

pigs

cows

ducks

sheep

horses

chickens

fish

cats

Draw lines.

10 farm animals

1. dog
2.
3.
4.
5.
6.
7.
8.
9.
10.

J ❤ : ______________________

Find the animals and write the words.

What have animals got?

	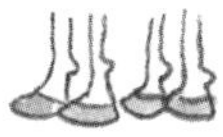 4 legs	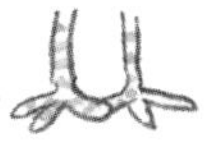 2 legs	 wings	 fur	 feathers	 tail	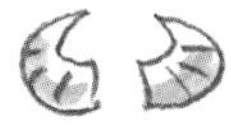 horns
cats	X			X		X	
sheep							
pigs							
cows							
horses							
chickens							
dogs							

Put a cross in the right box.

Baby animals

____

____

____

____

____

____

____

____

c	a	l	f	x	x	x	k	i	t	t	e	n	x
x	x	f	o	a	l	x	x	x	l	a	m	b	x
x	x	x	x	d	u	c	k	l	i	n	g	x	x
x	x	c	h	i	c	k	x	x	x	x	x	x	x
p	u	p	p	y	x	x	x	p	i	g	l	e	t

Find the words.

CD What pets need

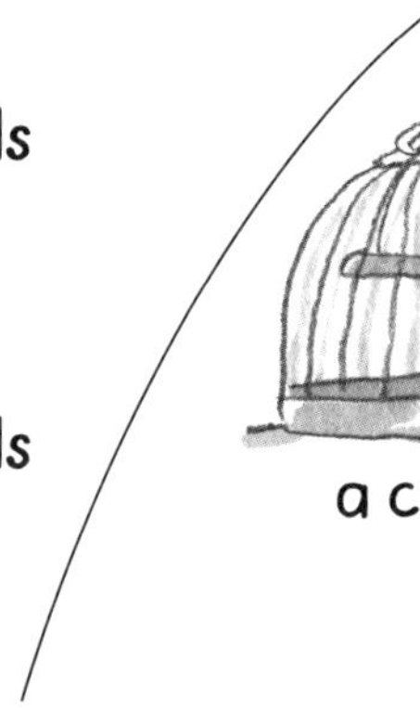

☐ A ______________ needs

☐ A ______________ needs

☐ A ______________ needs

☐ A ______________ needs

☐ A ______________ needs

a hutch.

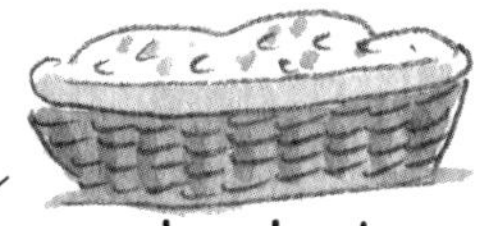

a basket.

a cage.

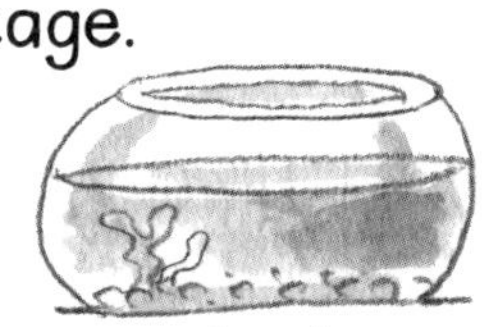

a tank.

a basket.

Listen and number, write and match.

My favourite pet

Draw your favourite pet.

A riddle

CD

corn

pig

four

pink

water

potatoes

short

She has got ____________ legs

and a ____________ tail.

She is ____________.

She eats ____________

and ____________.

She drinks ____________.

What is she?

What do you know about Miss Pinky Pig?

Who is it?

Kitty Kitten

________ has got ______________________________.

Molly Mouse

________ is ______________________________.

Peter Puppy

________ eats ______________________________.

Billy Budgie

________ drinks ______________________________.

Who is it?

Choose an animal. Write a riddle.

Sports and action

CD Reach for the sky

Touch your toes!

Flap your arms!

Reach for the sky!

Turn around!

Wiggle your fingers!

Jump up high!

Put your finger on your nose!

Clap your hands!

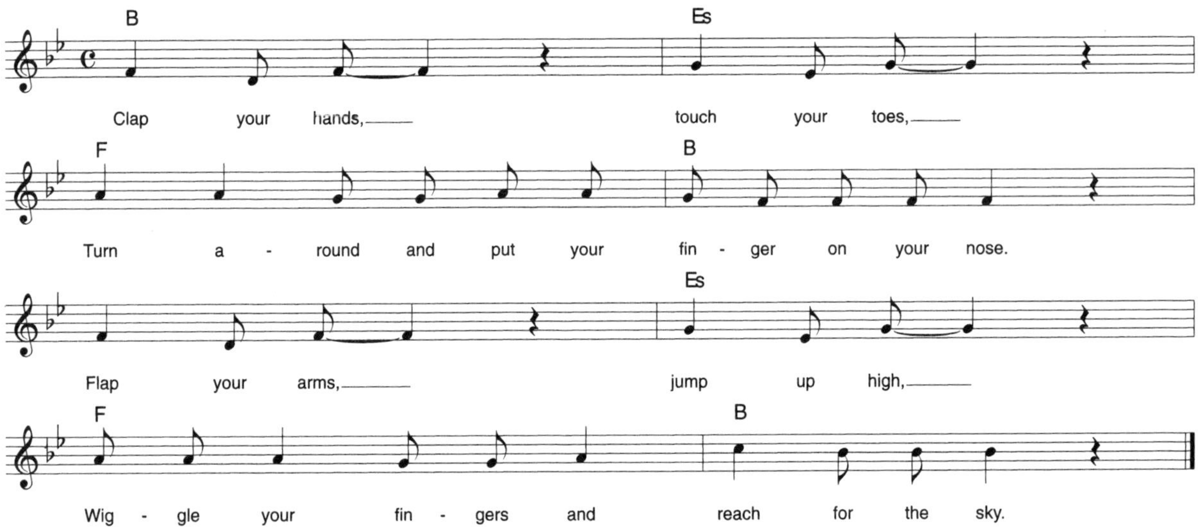

Find the matching pictures.

Sing the song and act it out!

Bumblebee's fitness plan

	FITNESS PLAN FOR: Bumblebee	how / long
1	skipping	40 x
2	running/flying	5 minutes
3	hopping on one leg	20 x
4	dribbling	15 x
5	jumping	20 x
6	stretching	6 minutes

Number the pictures.

My fitness plan

	FITNESS PLAN FOR:	how / how long / often
1		
2		
3		
4		
5		
6		

Create your personal fitness plan.

Sports on TV

I	X	T	E	N	N	I	S	X	X	Z
C	R	I	C	K	E	T	K	X	Z	X
E	X	X	X	X	X	X	I	X	X	F
*	X	Z	X	R	J	D	J	N	G	O
H	Z	X	Z	O	X	X	N	X	X	O
O	X	X	X	W	X	X	G	X	Z	T
C	Y	C	L	I	N	G	X	Z	X	B
K	X	X	Z	N	X	X	Z	X	Z	A
E	Z	X	X	G	X	Z	X	X	X	L
Y	B	A	S	K	E	T	B	A	L	L

basketball
ice hockey
football
tennis
cricket
riding
cycling
skiing
rowing

What is on TV? Find the words.

Sports highlights

Monday – Tuesday – Wednesday – Thursday – Friday – Saturday – Sunday

Day/Time	Channel	This week's sports on TV
Day: Time:	Sports TV	**FOOTBALL MATCH UK vs. Ireland** from Dublin
Day: Time:	BBC 2	**Tennis at Wimbledon** MEN'S FINAL MATCH
Day: Time:	Channel 1	European Swimming Competitions from Brighton
Day: Time:	BBC 1	**LONDON MARATHON** Many international stars
Day: Time:	Euro Sport	International Show Jumping from Edinburgh
Day: Time:	Channel 7	**Cambridge – Oxford** **Rowing Competition**

Monday – Tuesday – Wednesday – Thursday – Friday – Saturday – Sunday

Fill in the days and times.

What do you need for ...?

tennis	football	jogging
swimming	riding	
hockey	table tennis	cycling

Draw or write the things you need for the sport.

Birthday

Birthday wishes

Fill in the missing words.

Create a birthday card for your friend.

Take off with

Bumblebee

Me-Book

name: ______________________________

school: ______________________________

class: ______________________________

That’s me

my family:

my friends:

I like:

my fingerprints :

Saying hello

My classroom

Things I do at school:

I draw.

I write.

I read.

I count.

school bag

pencil case

ruler

rubber

glue

pens

computer

pencil

chair

book

blackboard

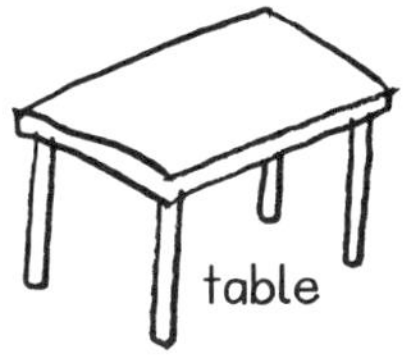

table

I play.

I sing.

Colours

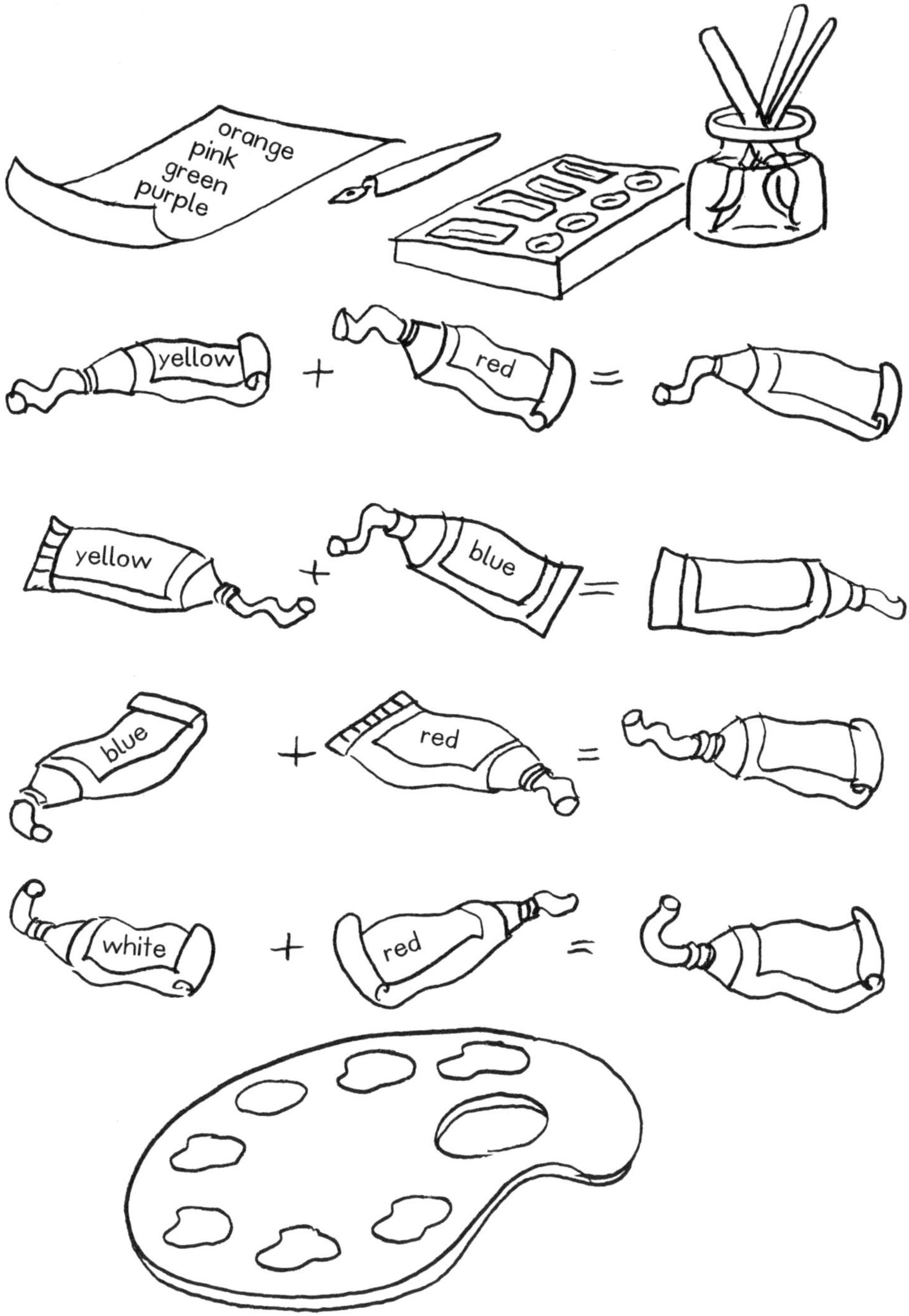
orange
pink
green
purple
yellow + red =
yellow + blue =
blue + red =
white + red =

My favourite colour

Clothes

pullover
scarf
T-shirt
skirt
gloves
jeans
shoes
boots
socks
trainers
dress
jacket
hat
woollen hat
cap
shirt
tie

Let us dress up!

Games, games, games

skipping

football

catch

hide-and-seek

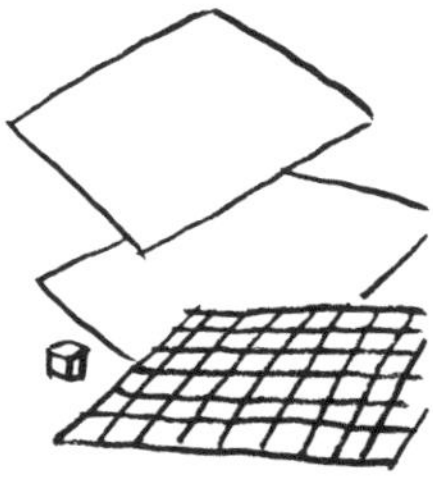

board games

hopscotch

basketball

table-tennis

Let us play together!

On the farm

Body parts

My farm animal

What pets need

hutch

lettuce

dog

guinea pig

fish

budgie

basket

I like ❤ : ______________________________

______________________________________.

hamster

rabbit

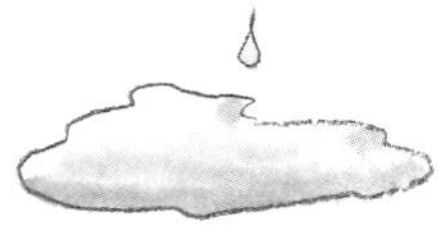

gerbil

cage

corn

need:

Sports and action

My favourite sport on TV

Birthday

H_ _ _ _ y b_ _ _ _ _ _day
to _ _ _
guests
flowers
birthday child
crown
Happy birthday
present
cake
card

My birthday calendar

January	February	March
April	May * Bumblebee	June
July	August	September
October	November	December

Fruit and vegetables

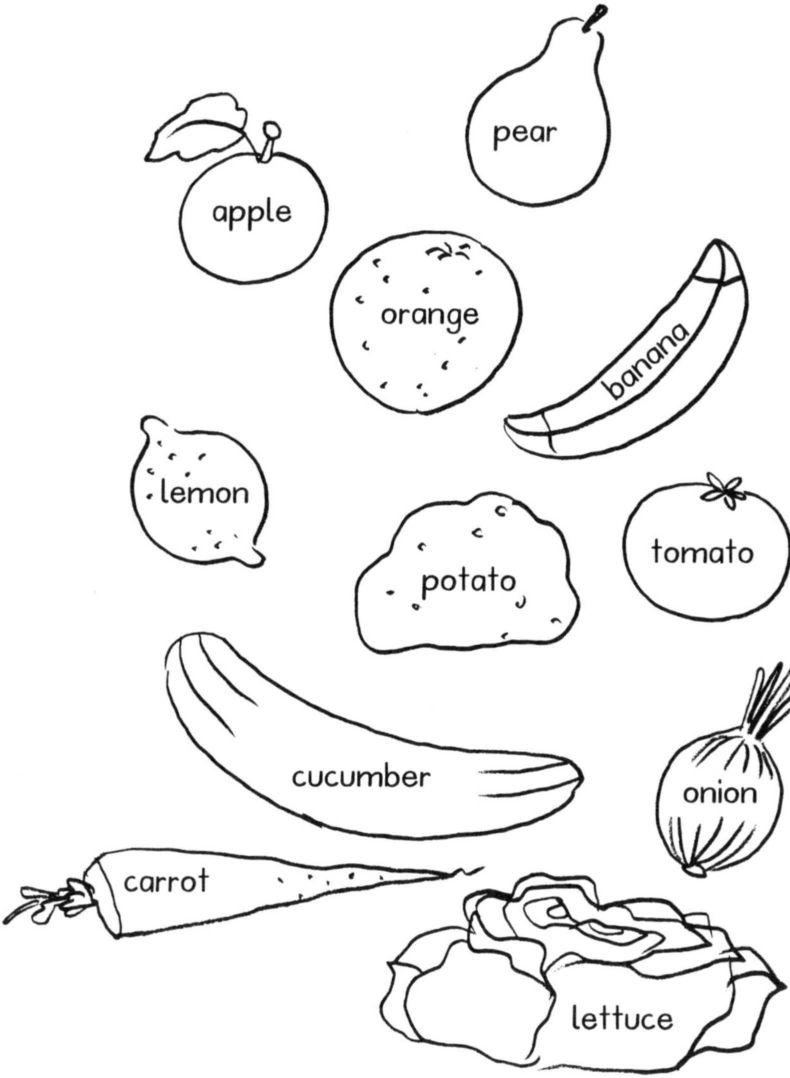

My shop

Dragons

on top of
next to
in

Postman Pete

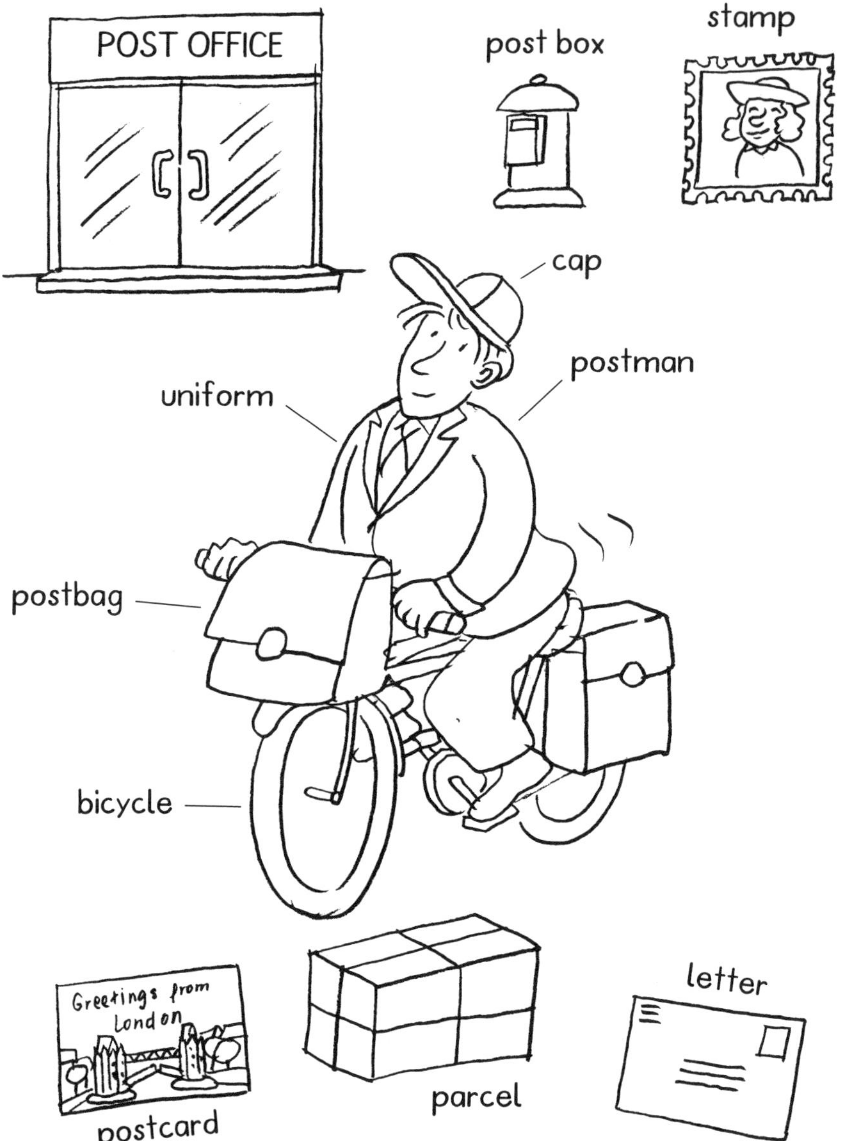

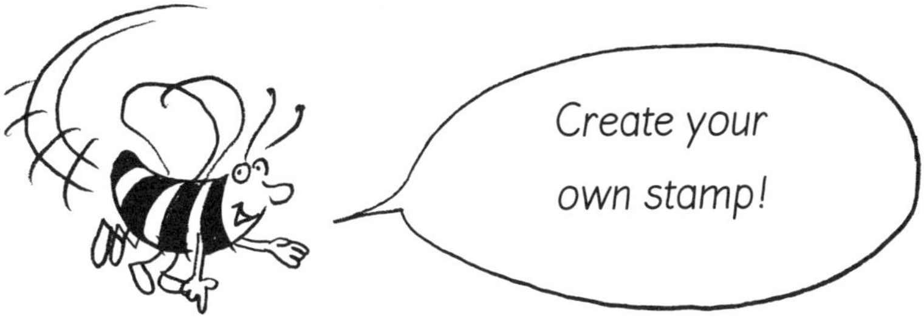
Create your own stamp!

Days, weeks and months

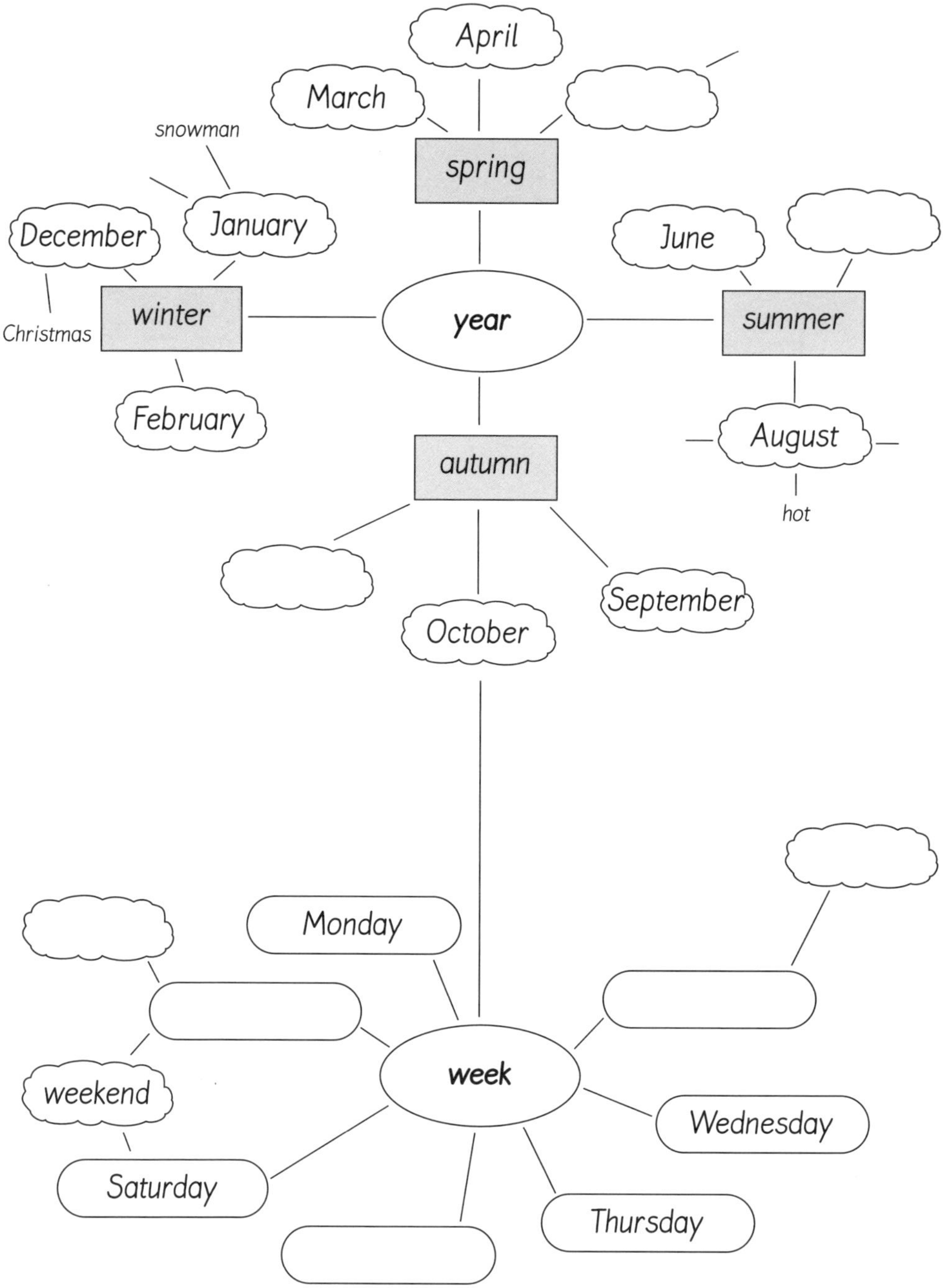

What time
is it, Sue?

Christmas

Father Christmas
Christmas present
Christmas tree
candle
star
Merry christmas
angel
Christmas stocking
Christmas card
bell
Christmas cracker

My Advent Calendar

12	7	10	20
19	4	1	8
Christmas Eve 24	15	17	21
	14	Christmas Day 25	
11	22	2	13
16	9	23	3
	6	18	5

About me

Meine Englischlehrerin heißt: ______________________

Auf Englisch verstehe ich,

- ☺ wenn sie mich begrüßt.
- ○ wenn ich dran bin.
- ○ wenn eine Geschichte erzählt wird.
- ○ wenn ich gelobt werde.
- ○ wenn ich etwas zeigen soll.
- ○ wenn wir Lieder singen.
- ○ ______________________
- ○ ______________________

Ich kann auf Englisch sagen:

- ○ Guten Tag!
- ○ Auf Wiedersehen!
- ○ Hilfst du mir bitte?
- ○ Danke schön.
- ○ Entschuldigung.
- ○ Ich bin dran!
- ○ ______________________
- ○ ______________________

Außerdem kann ich auf Englisch

◯ etwas über mich erzählen. Zum Beispiel: ______________________

____

____

◯ andere nach ihrem Namen fragen.

◯ fragen, wie es jemandem geht.

◯ Gedichte und Lieder vortragen.

◯ jemanden einladen.

Das kann ich auf Englisch am besten:

◯ Verstehen, was jemand sagt.

◯ Lesen

◯ Sprechen

◯ Schreiben

Meine Lieblingswörter zu den Themen:

shopping
seasons
food
games
colours and clothes
school
animals
Christmas
sports

Hello!

Weißt du, was du gerade in der Hand hast? Dies ist dein ganz persönliches Englischheft. Weil es extra für dich ist, heißt es Me-Book, also „ein Buch für mich". Darin findest du viele Wörter, die du mit Bumblebee lernst. Vielleicht kennst du zu manchen Themen auch Wörter, an die wir gar nicht gedacht haben? Dafür haben wir auf vielen Seiten extra Platz gelassen. Dort kannst du alles, was dir wichtig ist, hinein malen, kleben und schreiben. Am Ende des Schuljahres hast du dann dein eigenes Bildwörterbuch, in dem du deine englischen Lieblingswörter und -sätze finden kannst.

Viel Spaß beim Englischlernen!

Have fun!

Party time

CD

Act it out in groups of three!

Birthday words

crown
cake
song
guests
card
present
party
child
candle

Write the birthday words.

A birthday burger

Create your favourite birthday burger.

Shopping

CD Jimmy and Sally go shopping

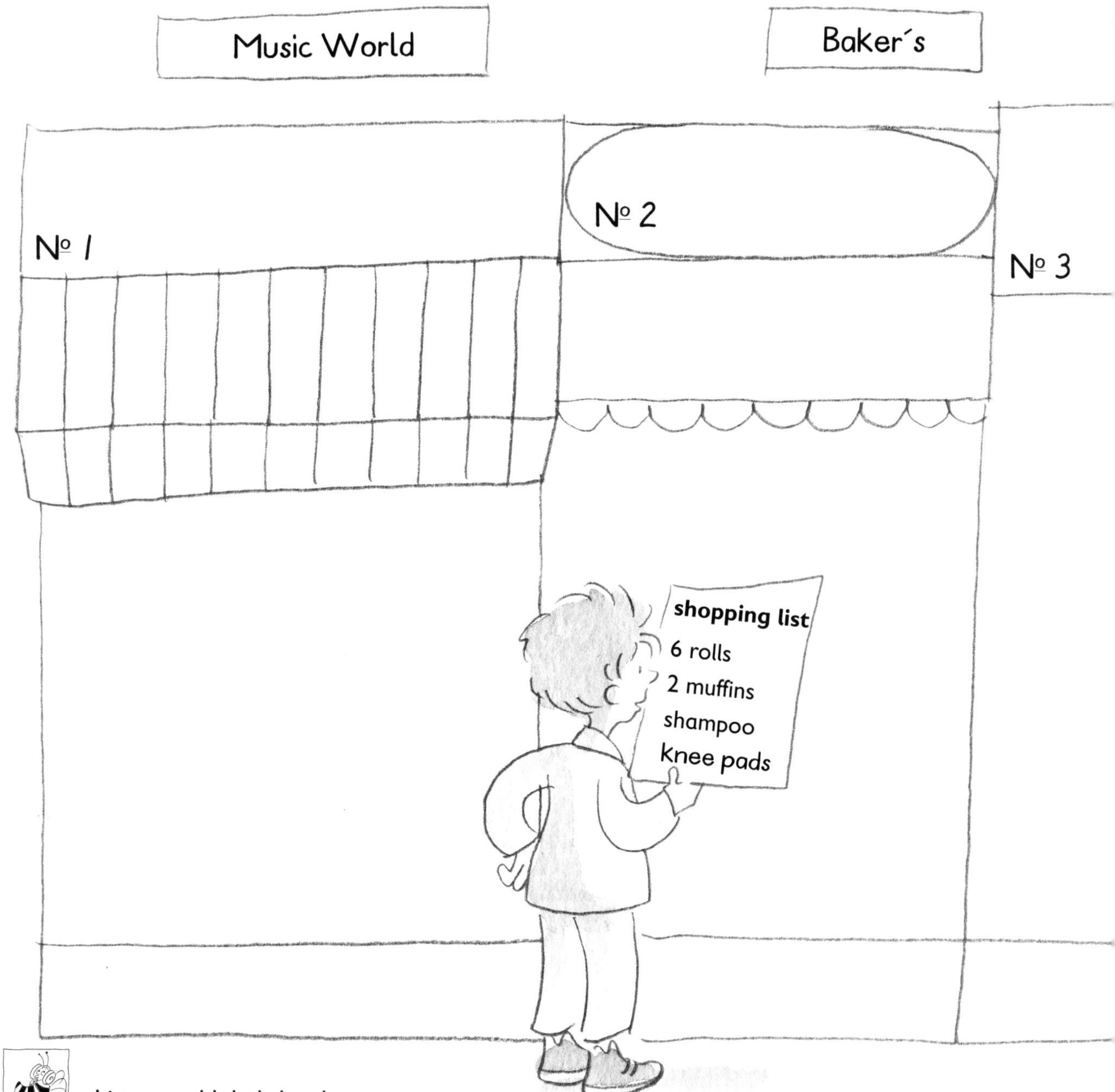

Listen and label the shops.

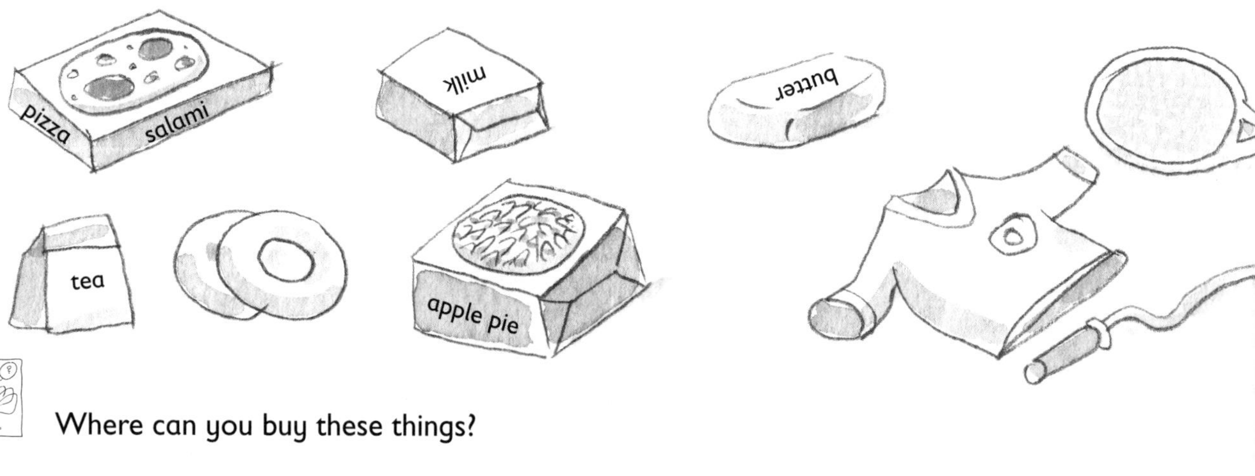

Where can you buy these things?

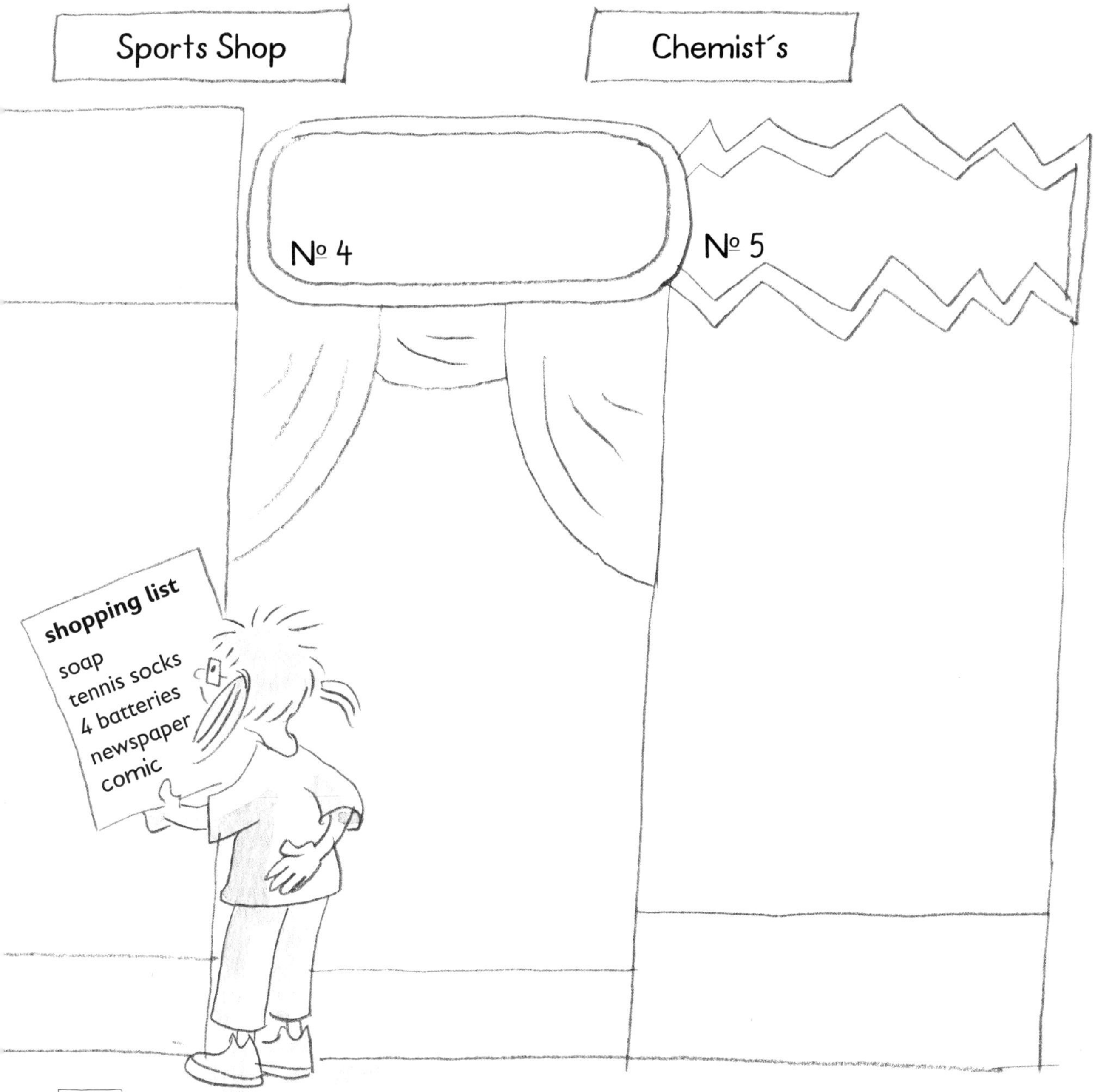

Help Jimmy and Sally to find the right shops.

Which shop is missing?

At the kiosk

Write the dialogue.

Money

How much is your change?

My shopping list for a fruit salad

Write a shopping list and make a fruit salad.

A lunchbox

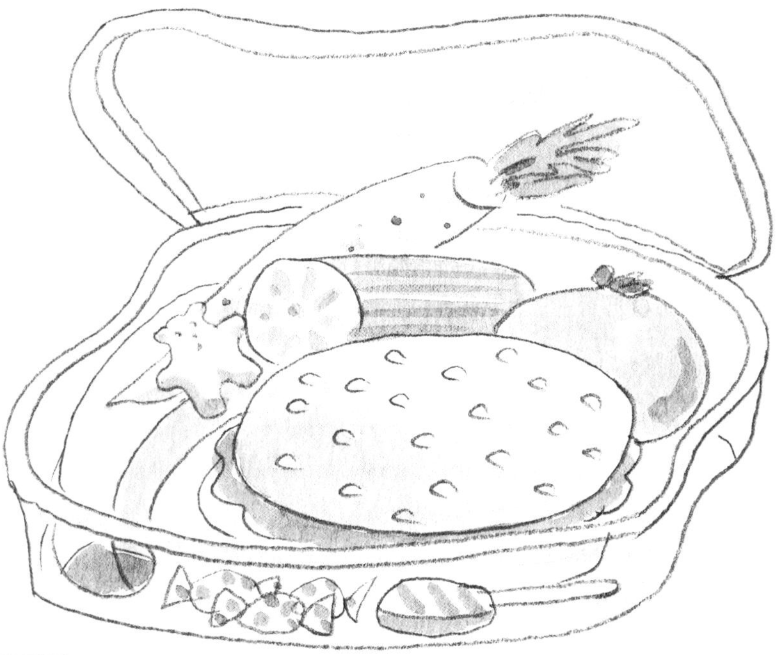

Colour the healthy things. Can you write them?

What have you got in your lunchbox?

Dragons

CD What dragons look like

Listen and colour.

A yummy, yummy dragon breakfast

salty	sweet	bitter	hot	sour

DRAGON MENU

____

____

____

____

____

Write a yummy dragon breakfast menu.

What dragons like doing

- writing
- drinking
- reading
- eating
- dancing
- diving
- playing
- swimming

Match the words with the right pictures.

Dragons can sleep anywhere

On the table.

Under the chair.

On top of the house.

Next to a mouse.

In an empty shoe.

Listen, match and play.

Draw the missing picture.

Dragon's lullaby

Where is Nessie?

Nessie is on top of the castle.
Nessie is in the castle.

Nessie is next to the book.
Nessie is on the book.

Nessie is on top of the castle.
Nessie is under the castle.

Nessie is next to the cow.
Nessie is on the cow.

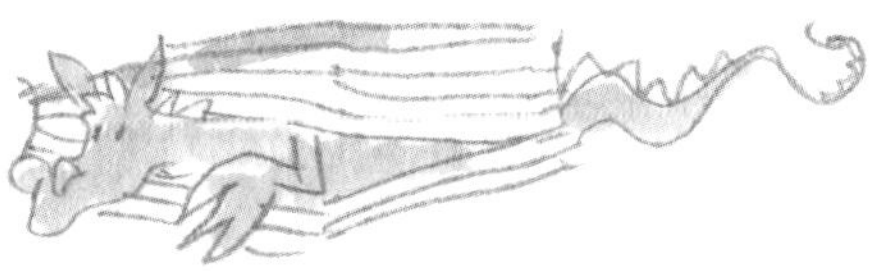

Nessie is in the book.
Nessie is under the book.

Nessie is on the cow.
Nessie is under the cow.

Find the right sentences.

Draw Bumblebee

on the sofa.

under the tree.

in bed.

Postman Pete

People at work

 Find the matching pictures.

 Who is missing?

Who needs what?

______________________________ needs a police car.

______________________________ needs a postbag.

______________________________ needs a baker's shop.

______________________________ needs a basket.

______________________________ needs a sign.

______________________________ needs a bus.

 Complete the sentences.

Postcards from Europe

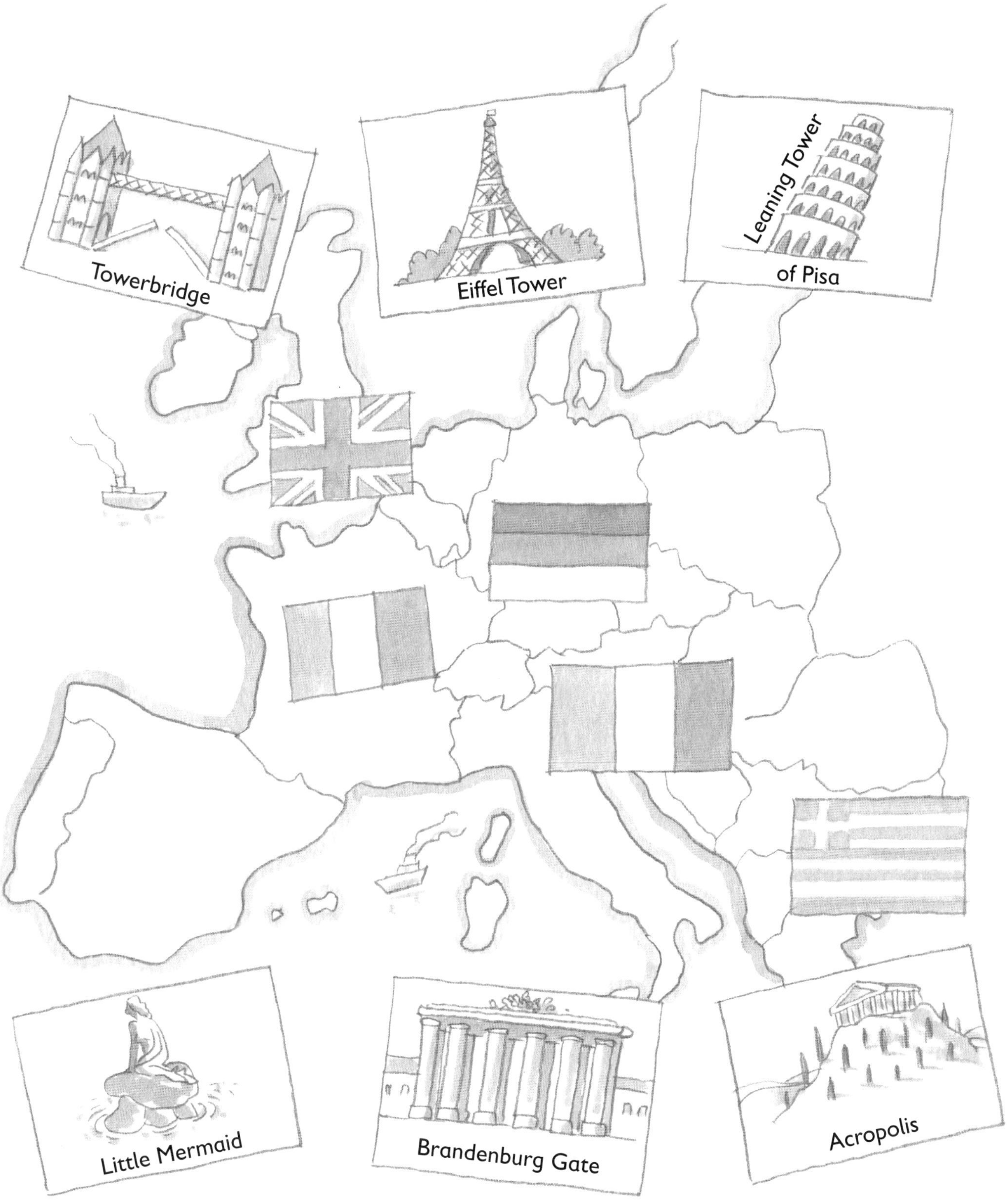

Where are the postcards from?

Colour the flags.

CD Here comes the postman

Here comes our  all dressed in blue.

Has he got a  for me or for you?

He carries his 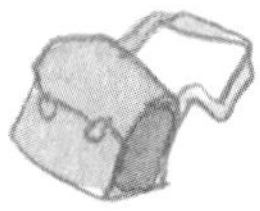

Through   or 

Brings   

and always says 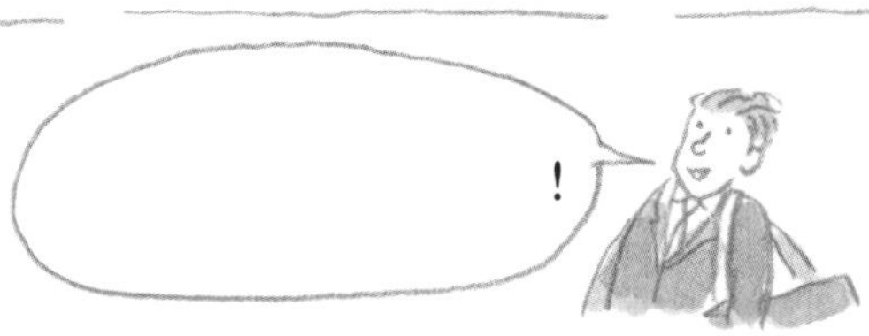

He knows a lot of  in our little  :

The  , the  , Mr Potter and Miss Brown.

 Try to read the rhyme.

 Can you write the words?

A postcard to Bumblebee

Stick a postcard
of your town

HERE!

To
Bumblebee

12 Honeyroad

LONDON

SE 1 0BQ

GREAT BRITAIN

Please write me a postcard!

Days, weeks and months

A calendar

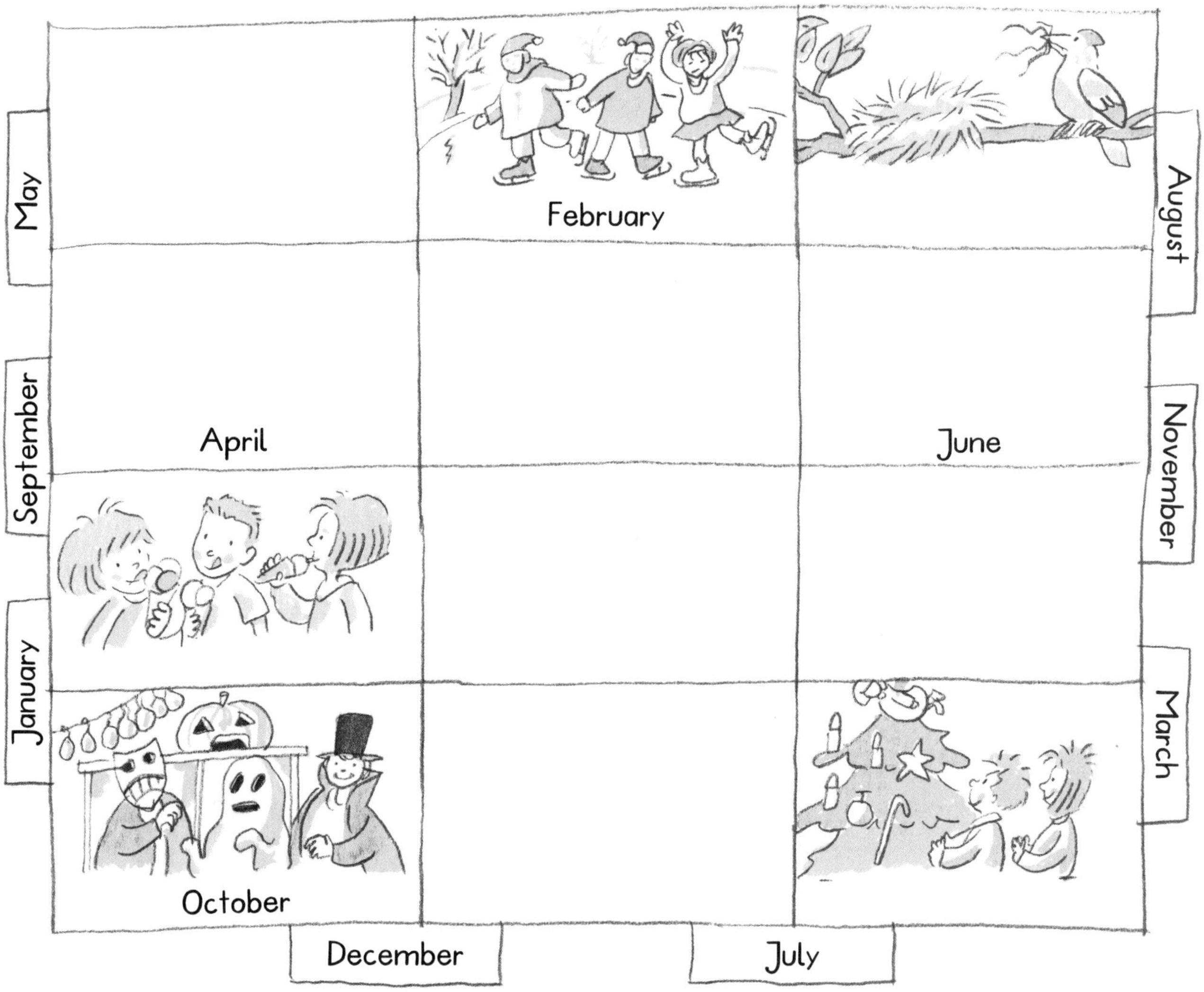

Complete the calendar.

Special days

My birthday is in ______________________.

Christmas is in ______________________.

Halloween is in ______________________.

______________ is in ______________________.

______________________________________.

Complete the sentences.

What time is it?

CD

Listen and number.

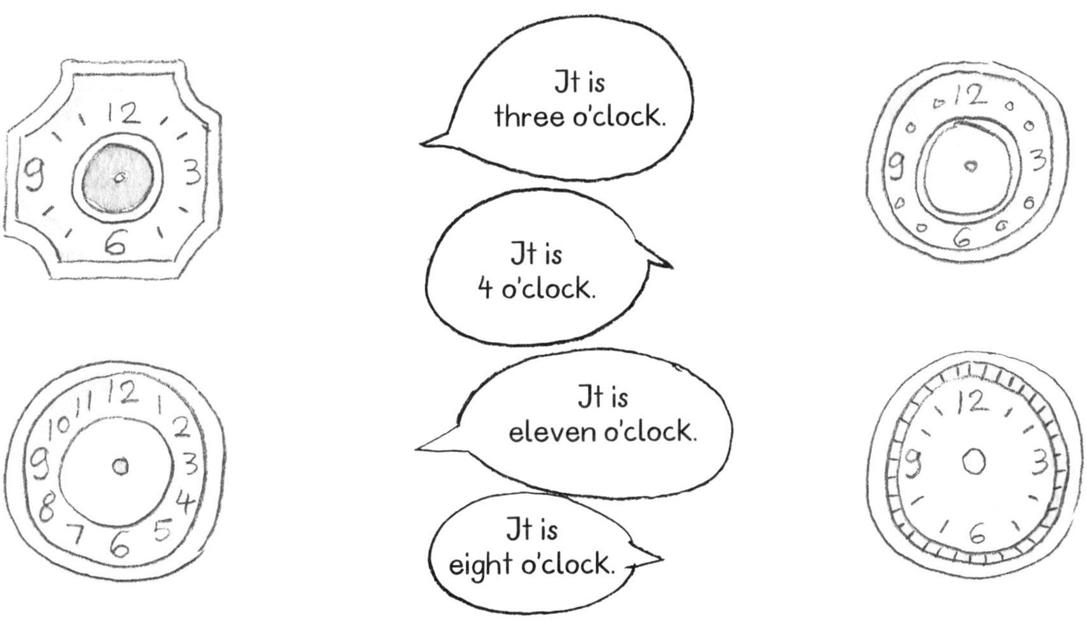

Can you draw the right time?

My busy day

1) J get up.

2) J go to school.

3) J have lunch.

4) J do my homework.

5) J play with my friends.

6) J have dinner.

7) J go to bed.

Find the matching pictures.

What about your day? Fill in the times.

My subjects at school

religions

English

P. E.

German

science

arts and crafts

swimming

music

maths

Match it.

My timetable

Lesson					
1					
2					
3					
4					
5					
6					

Write your timetable.

Christmas

CD Christmas dreams

Listen and number Simon's wishes.

Draw or write your Christmas dreams.

I hear them

CD

Colour the page in.

Sing the song in your class.

Christmas presents for my family

my presents for Mum:

____
____
____
____
____

my presents for ______________________:

____
____
____
____
____
____

my presents for ______________________:

____
____
____
____
____
____

Write your Christmas shopping list.

Odd man out

Christmas tree
Christmas stocking
Christmas shoe

Father Christmas
Uncle Christmas
Santa Claus

Christmas banana
Christmas present
Christmas turkey

Christmas Day
Christmas night
Christmas Eve

Mark the wrong words. The pictures can help you.

A Christmas crossword

Father Christmas
turkey
cracker
present
Christmas tree
stocking
decoration
card
star
candle
reindeer
angel

Do the crossword.

Classroom phrases

What my teacher says to me

Write it on the blackboard, please.

Bitte schreibe es an die Tafel.

Take out your exercise books, please.

Holt bitte eure Hefte heraus.

Open your books on page ten, please.

Bitte schlagt eure Bücher auf Seite zehn auf!

Have you finished?

Seid ihr fertig?

Sit in a circle, please.

Bitte bildet einen Sitzkreis.

Listen carefully.

Hört genau zu.

Everybody take a partner.

Findet einen Partner/eine Partnerin!

Try to say that in English. I'll help you.

Versucht das auf Englisch zu sagen. Ich helfe euch dabei.

Shut the door, please.

Bitte schließ die Tür.